Leadership

Techniques And Methods Of Proven Leadership That Will Help You Discover The Real Leader That Lies Within You

(Essential Actions To Take In Order To Achieve Optimal Outcomes In The Areas Of Motivation And Inspiration)

Avery Copeland

TABLE OF CONTENT

Introduction 1

How To Cultivate Positive Relationships At Your Place Of Employment 11

Both Inspiration And Motivation Are Included Here. 50

There Are Six Methods To Increase One's Knowledge In A Certain Field. 68

The Remarkable Rise Of Angela Merkel, Chancellor Of Germany And One Of The Most Powerful Women In The World 86

Some Real-World Applications Of Emotional Intelligence That Can Help You Lead A Better Life 91

Inappropriate Behavior In The World Of Business 97

The Dictation, The Tempo, The Pitch, The Tone, And The Volume 101

Strategies For Efficient Leadership Of Groups And Teams 109

The Driven And Enthusiastic Leader 121

You Really Need To Have Passion. 126

Social Skills 132

Theories Regarding The Continuum 142

People Are The Most Important Aspect Of Leadership 153

Educate Yourself On The Traditions Of The Working Environment 161

Introduction

It is not simple to get to the position of leader. The exercise of leadership is a significant obligation that, depending on the manner in which it is carried out, may result in a variety of outcomes. A good leader is someone who inspires respect and authority among his or her followers, who is sought to for guidance, and who acts as a positive role model for those who follow him or her. Everyone has the aspiration to rise up the ranks and become an effective leader, yet in their pursuit of this goal, they often make errors. Some individuals are naturally born leaders, having the required abilities and values already established in their personalities. Other people, on the other hand, have enormous potential in them to become great leaders but lack the motivation to work on these potentials. Both types of people have the ability to become leaders; the only difference is that some people are born leaders and others are manufactured leaders. This book will focus on the latter group, namely the readers who are interested in learning how to become effective leaders by making the most of their own capabilities.

I want you to save this title as a fast reference to have with you in those times when everything appears to be without meaning, and when others don't seem to understand what it is that you are trying to express to them. In such situations, I want you to take this title. Always look within, that is to say, examine what you are projecting outside via your actions, and this is something you have to do at all times. When you reach that point, it is imperative that you consult this book so that you may be reminded of the fundamentals of what it is that motivates individuals.

Norms for the efficient use of one's time

Get Started: The only things that are worth doing at all are the things that can be done properly. It is my opinion that you should begin each day with the first morning ritual, which is for you to get up early. This is especially true if you feel the need to successfully manage your time. When you have made up your mind to undertake anything, do not delay in getting started. The single greatest waste of time is procrastination.

Create a routine that serves as a guide for you: It's possible that adhering to a routine may prevent you from being creative, but in reality, doing so will only serve to familiarize you with that pattern over time, which will ultimately make it simpler and more efficient for you to find ways to work around such routines in the future. When you grow used to performing anything, you will find that it takes less time to complete as time goes on.

You will not be able to successfully manage your time if you take on too many tasks at once, so avoid doing so. Taking on too many tasks at once will not help you manage your time efficiently. It will prevent you from moving beyond the goal of pleasing other people./

Getting started on a work is relatively simple; however, seeing it through to its completion is where the real challenge lies. Leaving even a little work unfinished will just result in more time wasted when the task is picked back up later. Get started on a project and see it through to its conclusion for the last time.

You should avoid committing oneself to meaningless tasks, regardless of how far in advance they are: Making a commitment to a task in advance is not an efficient approach to manage your time and is also not recommended. Increasing your productivity may be as simple as doing one activity at a time on a regular basis. It does not matter how distant in the future it is; you will still need the same amount of time to complete it.

Separate enormous jobs into their component parts - enormous tasks should be broken down into its component parts as soon as possible. The bigger work may be broken down into smaller, more attainable objectives, which will ultimately lead to its completion. You will have a much easier time working it into your busy schedule if you take things one step at a time and tackle it piecemeal.

Make sure you give yourself enough time for each activity. Giving yourself enough time for each activity will help you maintain control over everything you do. This will need some guesswork on your part, but as you gain experience, your guesses will become more accurate. You and the other people involved will be able to better arrange activities as a result of this.

Make a plan for your endeavors: Planning is an efficient method for managing your time since it provides you with an approximation of what each day will look like.

Never put off doing what has to be done; all that needs to be done should be done right now. If you put it off until later, you will end up wasting even more of your time.

Your list of things to accomplish ought to be as concise as is humanly feasible. Any undertaking or exchange that is critical to your accomplishments should be given a certain amount of time to complete. You should make it a goal to spend at least half of your time engaged in the kinds of thinking, activities, and interactions that generate the majority of your outcomes. Prepare yourself for any interruptions so that when they occur, they won't throw off your schedule and cause you to lose valuable time.

Keep in mind that it is impossible to do everything, so you shouldn't be too hard on yourself if you don't succeed. The best way to improve is to practice.

How to Identify a Healthy Relationship and What Makes One

For there to be healthy relationships at work, there must be self-awareness, respect, inclusiveness, trust, and open communication. These are all very important considerations.

Have faith in. If you trust the people on your team, it will be much easier for you to be open and honest about your ideas, actions, and views. You may put your faith in them without having to worry about someone monitoring your back, which will allow you to focus your attention, energy, and time into increasing your output.

A sign of respect. Respect for one another is another essential component of healthy professional partnerships. When trying to develop answers, all members of the team need to appreciate and cherish the contributions made by one another, as well as the insights, creativity, and knowledge gained collectively.

To include. It is not just a matter of embracing those who have different viewpoints or those who are diverse. You are obligated to provide a warm welcome to them. When you are making choices, it is important to take into consideration the varying insights and points of view offered by other individuals.

Free flow of information. Communication that is both open and honest is the cornerstone of every healthy and successful relationship. The ability to communicate clearly and effectively should always be deemed crucial. Always keep this in mind whether you're in a face-to-face meeting, on a video conference, or even just writing an email. Because of this, you will have a greater connection with the team.

Awareness of oneself. It is important for every member of a team to accept personal responsibility for their thoughts and deeds. Nobody should have a bad influence on their coworkers owing to the terrible feelings that they themselves are experiencing.

Relationships at Work That Are Vital

It will be to your advantage to cultivate positive relationships with all of your coworkers, but professional connections should unquestionably take precedence over the others. One such example is the connection that exists between an employee and their superior at the place of employment. According to Gallup's research, the engagement level of a team may be determined almost entirely by the manager.

When a manager schedules consistent one-on-one meetings with their staff members, it helps to create and maintain positive working relationships. Employees benefit from these types of workshops because they get a better understanding of the role they play in the running of the firm. They will have the opportunity to get insight into both their capabilities and their limitations as a result of this.

You will be in a better position to work on the relationships with individuals who report to you if you take the time to study how your supervisor likes to work and try to anticipate his or her demands.

Developing positive relationships with important stakeholders may also be very advantageous to a project. These individuals include your clients, suppliers, and team members since they all have a vested interest in your success or failure. It is beneficial to your profession to cultivate relationships with influential individuals. The completion of a stakeholder analysis can assist you in determining who the most important stakeholders in your company are. After that, you will have the opportunity to invest some time in developing connections with them.

How To Cultivate Positive Relationships At Your Place Of Employment

It requires an investment of time to develop a strong relationship with another person. This is something that should be kept in mind in both your personal and professional lives. When you keep a few things in mind, it will be much easier for you to get along with your coworkers in a much shorter length of time.

Determine what each party in the relationship is looking for. Determine what it is that people need from you, as well as what it is that you require from them. Having this information at your disposal will be of tremendous help to you as you work to cultivate positive relationships.

Put forth the effort to build your people abilities. Having strong interpersonal skills is very necessary for the development of positive partnerships. You need to focus on improving your ability to communicate, as well as your ability to collaborate and resolve disagreements.

Train yourself to be emotionally intelligent. Having the ability to detect your own feelings and having an awareness of what those feelings signify are also very significant. When you put effort into developing your emotional intelligence, it will make it easier for you to comprehend the feelings of individuals in your immediate environment.

Improve your ability to communicate with respect. Never put someone on your team or anyone else you work with down in any way. Your relationships with other individuals may suffer if you have a caustic or nasty disposition. They will pick up on it even if you believe that you did not make it abundantly clear to them. Talking down to someone is a sign that you do not respect them and is something that person will notice and remember about the interaction. Even if you are higher up in the work hierarchy, you should never think that you have the authority to yell at others or behave impolitely toward them. It does not matter what position you are in; acting in such a manner is never acceptable. Your reputation as a leader will improve for the better if you maintain a courteous demeanor.

Listen with your whole attention. When you show that you are paying attention to what another person is saying, they will react to you in a more positive manner. Instead of always being the one to talk, make it a point to cultivate the skill of thoughtful listening. Figure out how to communicate better by listening more and talking less. People will see you in a more positive light as a result of this.

Make sure you schedule time in your schedule to create connections. Put forth the effort to strengthen your existing ties. Invite several of your coworkers to join you for a dinner or a cup of coffee. Leave a comment on one of their blogs, or just drop them a mail to see how they are doing or express gratitude for their work sometimes. These seemingly little exchanges will go a long way toward establishing a solid foundation for the connection.

Establish some limits. Even if you want to have positive relationships with the people you work with, it is important to establish clear limits. When a professional connection becomes too close on a personal level, it might interfere with productivity. You shouldn't spend more time engaging in social activities than you do really working, and you should urge your coworkers to follow your example.

Manifest your gratitude. Everyone enjoys having their efforts recognized and rewarded. Both your supervisor and the intern who is working under you are affected by this provision. People will experience feelings of pride and happiness when they are complimented on their efforts, so be sure to do so. It will not only inspire them to work harder, but it will also teach them to appreciate the good things you have spoken. The act of writing a few brief letters of gratitude will have a significant impact. Send a thank-you note to the individual who has impressed you with their hard work and good contributions at the office by writing them a letter to express your gratitude.

Keep an optimistic attitude. Make an effort to maintain a happy attitude as much as you can. People tend to gravitate toward people who can lift their spirits and make them feel good about themselves.

Stay away from rumors. It's possible to create a really toxic atmosphere at work by engaging in activities like gossiping and playing office politics. If there is an issue that you are having with someone at work, you should contact that individual directly rather than discussing it with another coworker. Also, avoid becoming engaged in issues that involve other people, since this will only have a negative impact on the connections you have at work. Avoid surprising your coworkers with unexpected news. They will feel as if they have been taken by surprise if they learn about an issue for the first time from another person, whether it at a meeting or from another supervisor. If you have a conversation about the issue with them first, it will lead to a more positive connection between the two of you. By sneaking up on your coworkers, you will destroy whatever chance you have of earning their trust and creating a productive network. If you don't have any allies, it will be difficult for you to achieve the professional objectives you set for yourself. Always remember to treat your coworkers the way you would want to be treated yourself.

Stay true to the agreements you've made. Work in an organization is inextricably intertwined at all times. What you do will have an impact on other people. Your failure to honor your promises or achieve your deadlines will have a negative impact not just on your own job but also on that of your coworkers. When you are unable to fulfill a promise, it is important to ensure that you have a valid justification for doing so and to provide your coworkers with an explanation. Put forth as much effort as you can to ensure that your promises are kept. If you are unable to fulfill a deadline, you should inform the people you are working with about the latest possible date you can finish the assignment. If you miss a deadline, you shouldn't automatically believe that you can get away with it without anybody noticing. Even if they don't bring it up to you directly, your coworkers will notice and take note.

Take part in activities related to social work. Participate actively with your coworkers whenever there is a gathering of any kind, whether it be a party, a lunch, or a conference. Make sure to introduce yourself to them and start talks with them. When you make an effort to connect with individuals in situations like these, they will pay more attention to you and be more forthcoming with information. In situations like these, getting to know your coworkers will be much simpler, and they will like working with you more as a result.

Don't place blame on anybody else. You will create a wedge between yourself and your coworkers if you continue to place blame. When an issue emerges, don't immediately point the finger of blame in someone else's direction. Even if they were the ones responsible for it, engaging in such behavior can only result in you gaining enemies. If you make someone appear bad by throwing them under the bus, that person will likely search for a chance to do the same to you. Creating enemies at work can only lead to troubles and ultimately lead to your professional failure. Instead, make further efforts to avoid such problems and build alliances with other people.

Give each other credit. Do not make the mistake of trying to claim credit for all of the effort. It is very important for you as a leader to recognize the contribution that each member of your team makes to the successful completion of a project. You cannot claim credit just for taking the lead. You will create a solid network with your staff as well as earn their trust and respect if you take the time to thank them, recognize them, and reward them. These individuals will only contribute to your success if you make the effort to show them appreciation and take the time out of your busy schedule to do so.

Assist other people in uncovering their own brilliance. Everyone have a unique set of abilities and strengths. Invest the time necessary to determine the capabilities of the individuals on your squad, and then encourage them to play to their respective strengths. Both your team and the project will get advantages as a result of this. It is beneficial to the business as a whole when people are given opportunities at work to develop themselves individually. Spend some time each day recognizing and praising the accomplishments that others have made. To contribute to the development of a pleasant atmosphere at one's place of employment, one need not hold the position of manager. Every employee will give their talents and aid in the achievement of the organization's objectives if they work in an atmosphere that is inspiring.

The Expectancy Theory, as Depicted in Figure 6

According to the formula developed by Vroom and given the name Expectancy Theory, if the future seems to be somewhat appealing, we are aware of how to get there, and we feel we will be adequately rewarded for our efforts, then we will be driven to take action. In other words, individuals will typically exert a great deal of effort to perform up to the standard that is required of them if they anticipate a favorable and desired consequence.

The degree to which a person believes that a certain level of work performance is feasible is referred to as their level of expectation on this matter. To put it another way, the question is, "Will I get the results if I put in the effort?"

If a person has a fixed mentality or a development mindset, as well as positive external social evidence, this belief or sense of self-efficacy will be stronger in that individual. For instance, the inner conversation may go something like this: "I have faith that I will be able to finish these actions" or "I can see other people putting in effort and getting results, so I can as well."

Expectation levels are influenced by a number of different elements, including the degree of difficulty of the work, the amount of assistance that may be anticipated from superiors and subordinates, the quality of the materials and equipment, and the availability of information that is relevant to the situation.

Therefore, when the manager is in charge of creating expectations, they have the ability to favorably affect expectations by articulating:

You will have access to all of the necessary materials, and this is something that you are capable of achieving. Here are some instances of individuals who are presently doing it, or who have done it in the past.

The concept of instrumentality provides a response to the question, "If I finish all of these tasks, will I get the reward?"

The brain is a goal-seeking mechanism, and when we do something worthwhile, we are rewarded with a substance in the brain called dopamine, which gives us a pleasant feeling of accomplishment. This pleasant emotion informs us that what we are doing is significant and should be done again in the future.

As a manager, one way to boost employee motivation is to describe the positive emotions that will result from the successful completion of the assignment. Remember to do something to make the folks feel good after the work is over if you want them to continue engaging in this habit. Praise, appreciation, and a simple "thank you" are all great ways to motivate people without costing anything.

To have valence, there must not just be a reward for effort, but it must be the appropriate kind of reward – and there is not a single solution that works for everyone.

Here is where your feelings should come into play. Valance is about how you will feel when you obtain the outcome; will you cherish the reward? Expectation was rational, but valance is about how you will feel.

Discovering what matters most to the people you manage or lead is an essential part of your job. Is it something that is extrinsic, such as money, promotion, free time, or advantages, or is it something that is intrinsic, such as satisfaction or a feeling of achievement? It is critical to get the support of your workers by convincing them that the job at hand is important.

Keep in mind the significance of frame of mind and motivation to human performance as you read through this book and put its plays into practice. It is also important to note that the following are issues that may demotivate your employees: • there is no clear career advancement; • the working environment is inadequate or hazardous; • there is a lack of leadership; • there is conflict.

Expectation and mentality both play a role in the process of framing behaviors, and I have included a checklist at the conclusion of this section to help you ensure that you are making the most of your influence and effect.

John was a new manager who had just been promoted out of his peer group to oversee the business-analyst group at his firm. This was John's first managerial position. Because he was such a talented analyst and, in the words of his boss, had "good people skills," he was promoted to the post of lead supervisor when that manager departed for a different job. However, John had received very little training on how to oversee or manage other people, and he was somewhat apprehensive about his ability to perform in this new job because of this. Someone who worked for him and who had applied for the position that John now holds was obviously dissatisfied with the result of the process. John had a number of close friends among the other workers who were now under his direction. As colleagues on the workplace softball team, they had experienced a great deal of camaraderie together.

John had internal turmoil as a result of his new employment, but he did not share this information with anybody else. He wasn't sure how to oversee his old pals, and, if we're being honest, he missed being considered "one of the gang." On the other hand, he was driven professionally, and this new post offered him not only a chance to further his career but also an increase in his compensation. He took advantage of both of these opportunities. At the conclusion of John's first week on the job as manager, one of his coworkers extended an invitation to happy hour with the rest of the staff. Even though he had consented to attend, he was nervous about it. He was aware of the likelihood of them imbibing too much alcohol and engaging in idle chatter about the several workplace reforms that were now in progress. On the other hand, he was concerned about projecting an air of superiority or being "too big for his own britches," as his mother used to remark.

John found himself trapped between two impulses, both of which pulled at him with the same amount of force: the want to be liked and to stay on good terms with people he now oversaw, and the urge to establish himself in his new job. Both of these desires pushed at John with equal vigor. The first few months that John was in his new supervisor post, his manager saw that he appeared a little conflicted and reluctant to lead his peers, and he questioned whether John was cut out for the job after all. John's boss was concerned about John's ability to lead his colleagues.

What exactly is going on over here?

Those who make the switch from contributing member of a peer group to supervisor often experience the same sensation of discomfort as John. This shift in the life of a leader might seem like an identity crisis since the new leader struggles to let go of the prestige and pleasure he or she formerly experienced as an expert while not yet completely knowing how to succeed in a new job. Additionally, the new leader does not yet fully comprehend how to excel in the previous role. But the disquiet that John felt was a consequence of far more fundamental forces than he was partially aware of at the time. These forces were working in the background.

Individuals are motivated to satisfy two essential wants within the framework of all relationships: the urge to be near (togetherness) and the need to be distinct (individuality). The degree to which we are able to meet both of these requirements in a manner that is healthy and necessary for us will, in the end, define the state of our relationships, whether they be professional or personal. John's inner struggle was a consequence of the tension that he felt between these two needs, which he now needed to learn to balance in a new manner if he was going to be effective in leading others. In order for John to be successful in leading others, he needed to learn to balance his own needs in a different way.

Attempting to Find a Happy Medium

The degree to which an organization's leader is able to strike a balance between the two essential principles of unity and individuality is one of the most important factors determining how efficiently the organization as a whole operates. This is because of the position that a leader has within the relationship system of an organization. The age-old proverb that "virtue is to be found in the middle" applies well to the situation at hand as well. A healthy organization, like a healthy human, is the consequence of finding the middle ground between being near without being entwined and remaining apart without becoming isolated. This is true for both the individual and the organizational level of health.

Having said that, it is not always easy for leaders to locate this happy medium, just as it was for John. In order to maintain connections in a manner that is both healthy and balanced, we need to have a clear understanding of how we typically operate when we are under pressure, in addition to making a conscious and purposeful effort to strike exactly the right balance with our many different stakeholders.

Take Into Account The Following Questions: When something doesn't go the way you want it to, does it make you want to entirely give up on a project?

Do you believe that someone will stick to their word if they tell you that they are going to make a contribution to the project you are working on?

Do you find that whenever you think about the different outcomes of a project or issue, your mind immediately goes to the worst possible scenario?

Imagine that you are driving along the highway when your vehicle suddenly stops working. Give me four reasons to be optimistic about the future because of that circumstance. Think about things other than your vehicle and yourself, such as the people you may encounter and the accidents you might have been able to prevent.

How to Increase Your Own Personal Accountability: People do not automatically possess the quality of taking responsibility for things in their lives. It is a talent that may be acquired by individuals and used to their benefit in the future. You may learn to take responsibility for the things you should be taking responsibility for by doing any one of a number of different things.

The first thing you need to do in order to be responsible is to have a clear understanding of your function. If you are uncertain precisely what your position is in the workplace or on the team that you are a part of, you should request that your duties be stated. This will ensure that everyone is clear and on the same page.

Putting aside your pride and being honest with both yourself and the people around you is another manner in which you may accept responsibility for the things that have happened. Instead of lying and attempting to cover up the errors you've made, accept what's occurred and utilize it as a learning lesson rather than lying and trying to cover it up. When you are having trouble, you also have the option of asking for assistance so that you do not let down others around you.

Don't let your pride prevent you from saying sorry. If you are to blame for anything that has gone wrong, you are required to provide an apology and make reparations. You are demonstrating that you care about putting things back in order by acting in this manner. Don't put off the activities that you don't want to perform right now; doing so will enable everyone concerned to move on and concentrate on the solution rather than the issue.

Procrastination is a typical strategy that people use to delay dealing with an issue in the hopes that it will be solved for them by another else. One of the simplest ways to be responsible is to find out what causes you to put things off and then use effective time management strategies to organize your day, prioritize your work, and complete the activities that are most essential to you.

When agreeing to take on a new responsibility, make sure that your schedule is taken into mind. When you take on too much, sooner or later, something is going to be lost in the gaps, and someone is going to be disappointed as a result.

Being responsible may provide you with numerous possibilities to expand your knowledge. When something doesn't turn out the way you expected it to, asking for feedback might help you figure out what went wrong and what you could do better in the future.

Think about it Please Respond to the Following Questions:

If things doesn't go according to plan, do you tend to be the first one to come up with an explanation for why it happened?

Do you anticipate receiving praise from others if you successfully complete a task or go above and beyond what is expected of you?

You are the head of a group that has been tasked with developing an end-of-season presentation for a customer. The purpose of this presentation is to show the client how well their product has been selling at the retail chain that you are employed by. You come to the conclusion at the end of the time allotted to you to finish it that there is some essential information that you have neglected to remember and that has not been included in the presentation. The presentation of the project was scheduled for the morning, but you have already finished working for the day. What are you engaged in? Do either of you remain late at work to finish it, delegate it to the person of the team who was expected to finish that aspect of the project in the first place, or do both of you stay late to make sure the material was included into the presentation correctly?

When your manager discovers that you are staying late at work, he will ask you what project you are working on that requires you to remain late. When he discovers that the material has been left out, he will ask you how you could have possibly forgotten to add something that is so important in the first place. What reaction do you have? Are you accepting responsibility for your actions as a result of your reaction, or are you shifting the blame to another person whom you believed was handling the situation?

A Guide to Improving Your Self-Confidence: It is essential for your success as a leader that you have a high degree of self-assurance in addition to a high level of expertise. It is natural to have periods of self-doubt, but it is equally essential to push over such periods and concentrate on the aspects of your personality and abilities that serve you well.

Stay focused on the facts. Keep in mind that the reason you are in a position of leadership is because you have earned it. Remind yourself of the reasons why you were chosen for the post. First things first: compile a list of all of your impressive abilities and achievements. You are free to read the list aloud or in your head, so long as the items on the list are truths about yourself rather than exaggerated compliments.

Find the issue that causes you the greatest self-doubt and challenge yourself to overcome it so that you can demonstrate to yourself that you are capable of achieving your goals. For instance, if you are most worried about having to communicate your ideas to your new team, you could practice doing so with a close friend or member of your family first. The next step is to carry it out in actual life rather than putting it off. You will get the increase in self-assurance necessary to realize that you are capable of becoming an excellent leader as a result of this.

Give yourself a speech of encouragement. Look at yourself in the mirror and act as if you are having a conversation with someone else. You should address yourself by name and say the things that you would say to a friend or colleague if they confided in you that they were anxious about the same things that you are anxious about.

Think About These Questions: When you're going into a scenario for the first time, what emotions often go through your head? How do you feel about it when it's over?

What are some of the qualities that you possess that make you an excellent candidate for a leadership role?

Do you use terms that are positive and encouraging when you describe yourself, or do you minimize the accomplishments that you have achieved? Do you exaggerate your achievements in order to give the impression that you are more successful and self-assured?

When you go in for a job interview, do you enter with the mindset that you are going to get the job, or do you enter the interview uncertain of whether or not you are qualified for the position?

How to Develop Your Ability to Make Decisions: Some individuals have a natural tendency to make decisions, while others have a natural tendency to avoid making decisions. There are actions you can do that will help you become a person who is more decisive and willing to take on a leadership position even if you are someone who is naturally unable to make decisions.

Do not give yourself or others the impression that you are unable to make a decision. Rather than that, you should reassure yourself that you are determined. Not that you will be or even that you are capable of becoming. Tell yourself that you are able to make choices and that you can firmly stick to them. Also, tell yourself that you are decisive.

You shouldn't be concerned about the possible poor choices you may make. Instead, recognize that every choice you make presents you with a chance to learn something new. Having an awareness of the positive aspects of a decision, even if it leads to an undesirable conclusion, may help you feel less anxious about the prospect of making a choice that will have unfavorable consequences.

Recognize that one of the decisions you are making right now is to not make a choice at all. Something is going to take place regardless of whether or not you have made a conscious decision for it to do so. You cede control of the circumstance to another party when you choose not to make a choice in the matter. In the end, it will be to your advantage to make the choice on your own rather than to let power slide through your fingers.

Think About These Questions: Do you spend time worrying about what other people are going to think of the choices you make?

When you reach a conclusion, do you choose the option that you believe would be most advantageous to your team, or do you choose the one that you had to choose because you were pressured into it?

When you reach a conclusion, do you have full faith that it was the best option, or do you often find yourself wishing you could change your mind and start over?

As a leader, do you make choices on your own, or do you defer all decision-making to the team and what they believe is best for the project?

A Guide to Raising Your Consciousness: A significant component of effective leadership is having an acute awareness of the dynamics at play inside one's workplace and among one's teammates. Even though many individuals go out of their way to avoid office politics and drama, it is important to be aware of these things from time to time since it may help you have a better grasp of the workplace and the dynamics of the team.

Make sure that everyone on your team has a good understanding of the direction that you want to lead the team in. Be conscious of the fact that a team that is well-informed on the objectives that have been set for them has a greater chance of achieving those objectives.

It is imperative that you refrain from elevating your own personal objectives to a status that is on par with those of the business for which you work. Your company's objectives are necessary, but they must not be in direct opposition to the objectives of the organization.

Keep in mind the conflicts that are really worth fighting for. Fighting every battle may give you a sense of accomplishment, but doing so will also give others the impression that you are belligerent and unyielding.

Be aware of how others see your abilities as a leader. When others fear you, it lowers the likelihood that they will turn to you for help when they need it. If others like and respect you, it is more likely that they will go out of their way to help you, especially if they believe that you will appreciate their efforts and reward them in some way, even if it is only with praise.

Take into consideration the questions that follow:

How would you describe the atmosphere at your place of business? Does everyone get along with one another, and is there open communication? Are you familiar with the members of the team who serve as managers, leaders, and other important roles?

How does your team generally feel about you? Do they treat you in the same manner that they expect to be treated by you? Are they straightforward and honest with you as a partner?

If you are in the process of recruiting a new member for your team, do you focus more on that person's talents, how well they will get along with the other members of your team, or a mix of the two? Why?

Putting the aforementioned advice into practice will not only help you become more focused and driven, but it will also improve your ability to motivate your staff. In addition to the things that you may do to improve a particular ability, the following are three more things that you can do to improve your overall effectiveness as a leader:

Determine the areas in which you lack strength so that you are aware of where you should focus the majority of your efforts;

Honor everyone on your team for all of their hard work and success. This does not imply anything substantial each and every time, but even something as simple as buying everyone a box of doughnuts to celebrate reaching a modest objective may go a long way toward establishing a positive image of you as a capable leader;

Communicate with your team, listen to the ideas they have, and figure out what drives them to perform at their highest level. If you take the time to get to know your teammates as individuals, the members of your team will respect you more as their leader.

Both Inspiration And Motivation Are Included Here.

The ability to inspire people demonstrates that you care about the success of your team. Those that work with you will be more likely to follow your lead if you can motivate and inspire them. To motivate individuals, you need to have compassion. Always keep in mind the thoughts and emotions of the people around you in order to have a better understanding of the requirements they have. Mastering the ability to inspire and encourage people expands your sphere of influence. You should both encourage your coworkers and employees to continue pursuing their goals and support them as they work toward achieving them. It is necessary to be aware of the motivations of other people because you must always be conscious of the fact that everyone who works with you works with the objective of achieving their own goals and satisfying their own requirements. Being aware of the motivations of other people is crucial. Your colleagues and coworkers will likely lose motivation when confronted with challenges and obstacles the majority of the time. They may also experience feelings of exclusion or frustration if they are required to do duties that are monotonous or repetitive. Maintain awareness of the happenings and circumstances that are pertinent to your team, and pay attention to the signs that indicate when some of your most valued team members are becoming dissatisfied. After this has occurred, do an assessment of their circumstances and make it a priority to give assistance in advancing their career.

Facilitate the Autonomy of Others

Your following will grow if you educate yourself on how to give yourself more authority. Because your success as a leader is contingent on the efforts of others, you should make it a priority to maintain a positive attitude and instill self-assurance in those around you at all times. This also entails concentrating on the good aspects, rather than the negative aspects, of other people and providing positive comments on a regular basis. In addition to this, make sure that you assign work effectively and involve your colleagues in any activities that are necessary. This will guarantee that each and every one of them is given the chance to grow their careers and accomplish their goals, therefore earning your respect and gaining your believe in their capabilities.

Acquire the Habit of Taking the Initiative.

This may be accomplished by participating in voluntary work and taking on more tasks. This will allow you to not only develop additional skills and become more competent within your domain, but it will also increase your presence and your sphere of influence. As you progress in your career and take on more responsibility, you will find that your knowledge expands. On the other hand, this firmly defines you as a successful leader within the context of your team.

Resolution of Conflicts

The capacity to mediate and settle disagreements is a crucial skill for every successful leader to possess. You should not overlook any disagreements or unpleasant circumstances that arise within your team but instead work toward resolving them in a way that is suitable. Listening abilities of a high caliber are required for this task. Listening abilities are very necessary for any successful leader. Learning how to listen involves not just picking up on the messages and feedback that other people are trying to convey, but also picking up on their motivation, state of mind, and maybe even their covert objectives. In the workplace, disagreements are often inevitable. An successful leader, or someone who aspires to become one, understands how to manage disputes and assist everyone concerned in coming to a settlement that is acceptable to all parties involved. This is true regardless of one's position within the conflict or their perspective on the topic. Even while disagreements have the potential to result in unfavorable consequences and damage relationships, they also have the ability to assist identify chances for personal development and advancement. In any case, acquiring the skills necessary to handle conflicts is essential if you want to improve your career and be a successful leader. According to Smiley (2018), a good leader has the option of choosing between two desirable approaches to handle disagreements, which include the following:

Cooperative effort.

Reviewing the stances taken by all parties engaged in a problem as part of a collaborative effort to resolve it may turn a contentious issue into a scenario in which everyone comes out ahead. After a disagreement has arisen, it is essential to go back and consider the perspectives and worries of all parties involved. Although doing so requires a significant investment of time and effort, the end result will be a solution that will be acceptable to all parties. In order to do this, you will need to make it very obvious that the primary objective is not to gratify aspirations or egos, but rather to fulfill the criteria of the position. First things first, you have to make sure that everyone's concerns are heard, and then you have to evaluate their rationale and explanation. After then, everyone who took part in the argument has to consider the potential advantages and disadvantages of adopting or rejecting a certain concept. This implies that you, as a member of a team and a leader, need to examine everyone's ideas for addressing the issue and provide the group with a review of what will be potential good and bad impacts from acting or not acting on a given assumption, concept, or choice. In addition, you need to present the group with a review of what will be possible outcomes based on the ideas that have been presented. This needs providing responses to the following four significant questions:

In what ways would taking action on the situation be beneficial to everyone involved?

What are the consequences that would result from taking action on the matter?

What are the potential advantages of being inactive with regard to the matter?

What are the potentially disastrous consequences of choosing to do nothing about the situation?

You will then be able to draw conclusions regarding the next measures to take based on the results that the team has uncovered. Accepting the proposals that have the potential to provide the most good results and the fewest undesirable ones should be the first step.

Make a concession.

There may be times when the team will be unable to come to a decision that is supported by all of its members. In this scenario, everyone will have to be content with a happy medium, or at the absolute least, they will need to meet each other halfway. Cooperation and assertiveness are essential components of this approach to problem-solving, which aims to partly address the requirements and worries of each person. To put it another way, reaching a compromise is finding a solution that is acceptable to all parties involved. In order for the group to be successful in their efforts to reach a consensus regarding the matter, they will need to devise a

strategy that allows them to bridge the gaps that exist between the various concerns and decisions that have been made by concentrating on the following: the urgent and high-priority demands of the work; the best interest of the organization; the best interest of the parties involved; and the best interest of both short-term and long-term goals.

When trying to create correct estimates of possible gains and losses, it is always a good idea to welcome the aid of competent consultants, managers, financial advisers, and other specialists in the field.

Integrity in the Rating Process

Being impartial and unbiased in one's assessment of one's own work as well as that of others is what it means to evaluate work fairly. Thinking critically is necessary in this situation. Fostering an autonomous mind is essential to critical thinking and essential to becoming a critical thinker. It involves providing an interpretation of the material that goes beyond its simple, literal meaning. This will save issues from developing and put you in a position to make the most of possibilities when they present themselves. To begin, if you want to be objective in your assessments, you'll need to work on increasing your ability to actively listen. Your capacity to accurately perceive the signals that other people are trying to convey may be improved by practicing active listening and observation of circumstances, group dynamics, and body language. When you are working on numerous projects at once, this is an especially critical consideration to make. Maintaining eye contact with the person you are listening to, avoiding any distractions, and making sure that your answer is relevant to the message that is being given are all components of active listening. According to Leskiw and Singh (2007), a significant portion of communication is carried out via the use of nonverbal indicators. As a result, it is necessary to acquire the skills necessary to recognize and decipher nonverbal language.

In order to go up in the ranks and establish yourself as a reliable leader, you will need to deliver fruitful outcomes. A person who is merely extremely ambitious may never be considered a real leader since they lack not only the skill and potential but also the appropriate competence. In order to do this, you will endeavor to build a reputation for yourself as someone who is objective and logical in the judgments and assessments they provide.

The following are characteristics shared by just leaders:

Leaders that strive to be fair refrain from being unduly domineering and dominating of their followers. In order to do this, you will need to let go of a controlling mentality and work toward aligning the expectations and interests of the team.

A leader who is fair is one who is also committed to equality and is impartial in their assessment. Being committed to equality requires conducting oneself in a manner that accords the same level of esteem and regard to all individuals. It involves taking into consideration the viewpoints and thoughts of all individuals. Your colleagues, coworkers, and acquaintances should be recognized for the valuable contributions they have made and the distinctive abilities they possess. Having said that, this also necessitates taking into account the unique qualities of each individual and ensuring that everyone has an equal chance to exhibit their skills. This also needs hard effort in observing and identifying the distinctive abilities possessed by each individual.

A person of integrity who is constant in their beliefs, values, and deeds is one of the characteristics of a fair leader. This necessitates tackling everything with sound reasoning and complete candor. A just leader is one that admits their own shortcomings, is honest about the challenges they face, and is forthcoming about the information they lack.

Aside from that, a good leader is someone who behaves in a way that is inclusive. A good leader does not focus on advancing their personal agenda or ambitions; rather, they concentrate on uniting their followers behind a shared vision for the future. This entails incorporating the thoughts and viewpoints of everyone involved and demonstrating a willingness to take into account the perspectives of all parties.

One other quality that exemplifies a just leader is the ability to command respect. Maintaining a respectful approach in communication can help to build a secure working environment in which individuals are free to express themselves freely and participate to the fullest degree possible.

It is necessary for you to abstain from some activities that are often seen as unethical by both your employees and your colleagues in order to further enhance your image as a leader who is fair. This involves, for personal reasons, choosing to ignore the negative behaviors of others while at the same time holding individuals responsible for their actions. If you try to avoid providing your colleagues and employees with criticism that is honest, this is another reason why they may see you as someone who is unjust. It doesn't matter what your perspective is; you should still recognise the outstanding job that others have done. The vast majority of colleagues despise it when managers show favoritism to certain employees. When it comes to sharing information and making significant choices, leaders that give priority just to certain of their staff members can seem as unprofessional and arrogant to their followers. This involves giving some members of the group preferential treatment over others in terms of the assignments of tasks, the allocation of your time, and the cash benefits.

You will, on occasion, run across circumstances in which the effort and dedication of a person are not rewarded with the outcomes that they had hoped for. In this situation, you need to be steadfast in your commitment to working in the organization's best interest rather than following your own personal inclination. In addition, a fair assessment does not imply forcing equality at any cost at any point in the process. When it comes to assigning responsibilities and awards to the members of your team based on their level of skill and productivity, you should always maintain a sensible approach. In addition to ensuring that everyone is treated equally at your place of business, you should also make it a point to recognize and commend employees whose efforts provide positive results and to discipline those whose performance falls short of expectations. When conducting rational assessments, it is important to take into account whether or not your words and actions are consistent with one another. What this implies is that the beliefs that you advocate for should be reflected in the activities that you do. In conclusion, but certainly not least, it is essential to provide sincere acknowledgment and credit, regardless of one's own thoughts, in order to inspire and retain the most outstanding individuals of a team.

There Are Six Methods To Increase One's Knowledge In A Certain Field.

1. Individualized Instruction

There are many different avenues open to you to learn more about your chosen field of work. The first approach that we are going to investigate is self-education. Self-education refers to the process of acquiring new knowledge by oneself via self-study and the collection of information in one's own self-directed manner.

Educating oneself on one's own may take many different kinds. Self-education is something that may be practiced by those who spend time reading trade publications, books, articles, and online blogs.

This individual is current on all the alterations and new technologies that have been introduced in their sector. They are able to make informed judgments because they are aware of what is currently relevant and what has been shown to be successful.

Self-education is advantageous since it does not need financial outlay. Investing in one's own education in this way requires a minuscule amount of time and effort. To get the necessary materials, one may make use of the resources provided by their employer, the internet, or a local library.

Self-education is really the most important type of education since it maintains our level of expertise and ensures that we are constantly on the leading edge of our field. If we continue to educate ourselves, we will continue to mature and become better at carrying out the duties associated with our leadership roles.

This sets an example for our subordinates to follow, which is really beneficial. Share with others some of the books and articles that you have read that have proven to be helpful to you in your line of work. Make it possible for other people to advance with you. People have a tendency to want to keep their information to themselves out of the concern that it could be used by someone else.

When people you lead succeed, it is a direct reflection of the time and effort that you have invested into their growth. This is especially true if you are in a leadership position. Learning to lead others requires not just one's own personal growth but also the growth of others around them.

It's possible to apply self-education to every aspect of our life. We can always discover resources to better where we are and learn more efficient methods of doing things, regardless of whether we work for a livelihood or are retired. This is true whether or not we have a job.

2. Education at an Institution

Formal education is the second kind of education that may be received. It's possible that your employer offers a program that will pay for all or part of whatever classes you decide to enroll in.

Why not take advantage of this education that is either free or offered at a discounted cost? This is a fantastic opportunity to educate oneself at no cost to the firm.

In the end, you and your business will come out ahead thanks to this. In addition, this demonstrates to your manager that you are interested in enhancing the quality of your work. A formal education may also help you discover more efficient techniques to use in your career as well as strategies to properly analyze the outcomes of your efforts.

There are several different pathways that may lead to a formal education. Consider all forms of paid informative situations as falling within this category of education. Trade schools, two-year colleges, four-year universities, graduate schools, conferences, seminars, and trade exhibits are all examples of possible educational opportunities.

Because they include the dissemination of paid information, we have decided to include items like trade exhibits and seminars. When you pay to attend a seminar, you are essentially enrolling in lessons in the subject matter that is being covered at the event. These are wonderful methods for staying up to date on what's happening in a given industry.

An official education is an excellent approach to expand one's information base. It not only enhances your qualifications but also has the ability to make you more desirable to your current company as well as prospective employers in the future.

Investigate the education policy of your organization and think about the ways in which you may profit from it. Think about the long term when you consider getting a formal education. People give much too much thought to the possibility that it will take them a number of years to get a degree.

They are only concerned with the quantity of time and labor that will be required to complete the task. The outcome is what we need to be concentrating on at this point. Ask yourself, "If I fast-forwarded two years, would I be happy in that future place if I had taken the time to get my degree or certification, or would I regret the time and energy I spent working toward obtaining my education?"

I believe that the majority of individuals who were asked this question would respond that they were ecstatic with the choice to seek higher education. The advantages far exceed the disadvantages, particularly if the expenses of your study are partially or entirely covered by your employer.

3. the role of a mentor

Mentoring is yet another fantastic technique to increase both one's knowledge and experience in a certain field. A person who acts as a teacher and a guide while another assists them in gaining expertise in a certain field is referred to as a mentor.

Mentors may be helpful in a variety of contexts, such as the world of business, the field of personal life coaching, the acquisition of parenting skills, the achievement of fitness objectives, the acquisition of a trade, the growth of a hobby, and so on.

You will never have access to anything that compares to the benefits that come from having a capable mentor at your side. This individual is able to supply you with the experience as well as the knowledge that you need in order to achieve your goals.

People never learn from their own errors, which is a significant flaw in human nature. Even when we are able to draw wisdom and experience from our past blunders, this is not the most efficient way to get experience and information. It is imperative that we gain wisdom from the errors committed by others in order to save ourselves from repeating those same mistakes.

One may gain knowledge and experience from the blunders made by a more knowledgeable and experienced person by having a mentor to assist them. Your mentor has the ability to guide you away from unwise decisions that you may have taken otherwise.

A good mentor will always keep your well-being in mind while making decisions. They will not pass judgment and will be upfront and honest in their communication. This is a significant point to make. A mentor should not be someone who continually brings you down by pointing out all of your mistakes or tearing you down on a regular basis.

A good mentor should be like the encouraging teacher or coach that you looked up to when you were a child. the one who inspired you to think that you could do what was placed before you was successful. They should support you, challenge you, understand you, willingly share their expertise with you, and have a genuine interest in your accomplishments.

The following is a list of some methods that may be used to find an effective mentor:

* Look for someone at work who fit the above criteria of a good mentor and who would be ready to assist you * Seek out a member of your own family who has expertise in the field that you are interested in learning more about *

* Hire a life coach or a mentor in a specific area of interest

* Seek out a former teacher or coach that you have a good relationship with and ask for their help

* Look for online mentor groups or opportunities

* Join an online community of people with similar interests who have already accomplished what you are looking to achieve.

4. Apprenticeship

The typical image that comes to mind when someone mentions an internship is that of a college student receiving entry-level experience in a corporation. It is correct to say that the majority of internships are organized in this fashion, but this is not the case for all of them.

There are businesses that provide their workers with opportunities to participate in internships or other comparable programs. This is particularly relevant in the event when an employee is acquiring a new skill set while still employed by the organization.

An internship is a fantastic opportunity to get experience and get your foot in the door of a reputable organization, and it is especially useful for college students. At the absolute least, it will provide you with valuable references and content that you may include on your resume.

You acquire hands-on experience in the industry in which you are interested in pursuing a career, which is yet another significant advantage of completing an internship. This is a really significant advantage. You could go into the internship with some ideas about the career that you ultimately want already formed in your head.

It's possible that after you've completed the internship, you'll be astonished to find that the position is nothing like what you imagined it would involve. This is a really significant benefit. It's possible that the job may reinvigorate your interest in the field you've chosen to pursue.

On the other side, you may discover that the work is very different from what you expected it to be. In this scenario, you have avoided a significant amount of stress as well as significant expenditures of time and money. You are free to pursue a different academic concentration in order to pave the way for a more appealing line of work.

If you hadn't participated in the internship, you may have graduated and started your new work without realizing how much you disliked it after just a year. Just consider how much time and energy you would have needed to invest in order to get to this conclusion.

An internship is not only an excellent approach to get knowledge about a new ability or career path, but it is also a fantastic opportunity to determine whether or not you will like the line of work that you will be joining in the future.

5. Making connections

Building ties with other people who operate in your sector or with individuals whose skill sets are essential to your success is an example of networking. Collaboration is working with other individuals toward the common goal of improving outcomes for all parties involved.

Building professional connections is an essential element of every career. Furthermore, it is of the utmost significance to our everyday life. Finding other individuals who share our values and interests may be beneficial to our careers, our businesses, our hobbies, and our day-to-day needs.

When we collaborate with other individuals, we not only raise our own level of consciousness but also draw from a pool of education, experience, and information that has been accumulated by the group as a whole.

Through building relationships with other people, we get the capacity to collaborate with those who possess specialized skills that we may be lacking. They could also offer ideas for potential solutions inside our industry that we haven't thought of yet.

Not only will this help you improve yourself, but it will also help the other person with whom you are networking. The ability to work together is essential to our success at the moment. If we work together to get more knowledge or to find a solution to a problem, we will be able to achieve a great deal more success than if we attempt to do it on our own.

The simple idea of forming professional relationships might make some people feel anxious. If you're an introverted person, I completely understand how difficult it is for you to leave your comfort zone and interact with other people.

You have to keep your eye on the prize. Are the potential rewards of emerging from your comfort zone more important to you than the risk of doing so? When we push through the unpleasant feelings we experience, we will mature and accomplish more than we could have ever dreamed possible.

Remember your final objective, take a few slow, deep breaths, and keep moving ahead. Fear might keep us from moving forward, yet having a strong desire to achieve something can propel us forward.

6. Past encounters

The best way to learn anything is via doing it, and experience is one of the best instructors the world has ever seen. When we get our hands dirty and have firsthand experience with something, we get self-assurance and a certain amount of comfort in what we are doing.

Find situations in which you can learn things via kinesthetic means. Instead of merely reading about the process in a book, put yourself in the position of really carrying out the routine or endeavor.

Gain wisdom from your past experiences and use those lessons to inform the choices you make in the future. It is important to keep track of the things you have learnt at all times. There will be far too many instances in which we will be presented with a learning opportunity, only for us to afterwards forget what we have learned.

Ask yourself, "What good can come from this challenge, and what lessons can I learn from this situation?" whenever you are faced with adversity in your life. It would be easier for you to confront the unknown and conquer difficulties if you think of problems and opportunities in terms of learning experiences.

You will emerge from this experience not just more wise but also more self-assured. Imagine for a second that there are two different persons dealing with the same issue. The first individual considers the prospects that may become available as a result of the difficulty. They attempt to extract as much useful information as they can from the event.

The second individual is hyper-focused on the challenges and issues at hand, making problem-solving their primary concern. They fail to gain anything of value from the experience and lose out on any potential advantages associated with it.

The first sort of person emerges from the test more experienced and more equipped to handle challenges of a subsequent nature. They now have a deeper comprehension and will be better prepared to steer clear of situations of a similar kind in the future.

The second individual has not learnt too much, and they are an excellent prospect for getting themselves into the same scenario in the future. They allowed themselves to concentrate on the unfavorable conditions rather than seeing the difficulty as an opportunity to develop their skills and expand their knowledge.

The sharing of one's experiences may also benefit others. The stories and experiences of the people around us may teach us valuable lessons. Examine every facet of your life and commit to maintaining an attitude of lifelong learning at all times. The more we comprehend the curveballs that life throws at us, the more prepared we will be to smash a home run.

The Remarkable Rise Of Angela Merkel, Chancellor Of Germany And One Of The Most Powerful Women In The World

For the eighth year in a row, she has been ranked as the most powerful woman in the world. Her strong suit is in being an outstanding and genuine leader. She upholds a moral code of integrity and demonstrates compassion for the people of her country. She is a strong advocate for her nation and its citizens. Her professional life did not begin in this manner, but she has since developed into a powerful, analytical, aggressive, and competent politician who proudly takes her place on the international stage.

Case Study 2: The Story of IndraNooyi's Triumph as Former Chief Executive Officer of Pepsi Co.

She was a firm believer in what she called the "five Cs" that women bring to the table: competence, courage, confidence, the ability to communicate effectively, and compassion. When questioned during an interview about what her exclusivity entails and how it has benefited the organization, she said that it is unique. According to a comment attributed to her, "Earlier it was driven by head, and I drove it with head and heart both." When you show empathy for the members of your team, it motivates them to provide their best effort and places their faith in you as a leader. It contributes to improved connection development and helps maintain good moral ideals.

"That's unbelievable! What is the most important advantage that the company will get from implementing diversity and inclusion initiatives?

Myra's response was that "Innovation" is the most important advantage. Having the capacity to perceive things in a new light is essential to innovation. The spark of innovation may be attributed to diversity and inclusion since it pulls together previously separate trends, such as globalization and shifting demographics. Sincere efforts are being made to integrate a diverse and inclusive workforce. The objective is to get at this point when there are not any male or female leaders, but simply leaders.

"Totally agree! Things have progressed noticeably in a positive direction. Thank you very much, Myra, for the really helpful information and unique point of view about the significance of diversity and inclusion in the working world.

She displayed a modest grin.

After we had finished talking, Aaron and Myra left the room, which gave me some space to think about what I had just heard. As I sat there in the peace and quiet, the question of whether or not I treated individuals differently just on the basis of their varied cultural backgrounds entered my thoughts. The attitude of a leader has to learn to accept and incorporate other individuals. I was reflecting on the many opportunities I've had to collaborate with individuals from a wide range of backgrounds in my line of work and how those interactions have helped me understand other cultures and provide superior service to my patrons. Sadly, I was never able to understand the situation from this vantage point.

My education in diversity and inclusion has equipped me with the knowledge to make conscientious efforts at work and to avoid falling prey to prejudice. As leaders, we have a responsibility to actively promote equality in the workplace, provide opportunities to those who are qualified, attract the appropriate level of talent to the organization, and make choices that will lead to success.

Some Real-World Applications Of Emotional Intelligence That Can Help You Lead A Better Life

Management of oneself as well as of one's relationships

When you have a high emotional intelligence, you are much more confident in your skills to regulate your own emotions as well as your interactions with other people. This confidence extends to your ability to manage your relationships with other people. This indicates that you have exercised managing your impulse control and been effective at doing so, and as a result, you feel completely powerful inside your own life. This may often result in a more favorable self-perception as well as increased levels of confidence and self-esteem. When you finally realize that you are the one in charge of your ideas and feelings, you will experience a marked increase in happiness.

This also indicates that you have built up a degree of confidence in yourself, which transfers into demonstrating to other people that you can be trusted. This demonstrates that you have a strong moral compass and that you are conscientious in the way that you think about things. You have experience in challenging circumstances that you have successfully conquered, and you are able to tell people about your experience with confidence because of it. It enables you to adapt to change because it makes you flexible in how you deal with things that have occurred to you since you are confident in your ability to manage yourself.

This level of self-assurance also endows you with the capacity to perform admirably in social situations. You originate from a place that is optimistic and adaptable, and you may utilize this to your advantage while engaging in discussion with other people. This is a genuine art form that is falling out of favor as a result of each new technological development. You will stand out as someone who is emotionally sophisticated and as someone who people want to speak to the more you engage in the activity and the more skilled you get at it.

Making Effective Use of One's Emotional Intelligence in the Working Environment

There are an infinite number of ways in which emotional intelligence may be effectively used to enhance one's performance in the job. Taking an honest assessment of both your professional skills and flaws is likely to be one of the most challenging but fruitful ways to achieve this goal. This is not meant to be a platform for you to criticize your own abilities; rather, it is intended to serve as a simple evaluation of the things that you excel in. You will also become aware of areas in which you have room for improvement; hence, when you get criticism in these areas, you will be able to properly take notice of it.

Find techniques to cope with stress in a manner that is good for your health and is acceptable for the situation. It is also crucial that you do this. To reduce the negative effects of stresses in your life, it is important to strike a healthy balance in your life by ensuring that you have time outside of work to engage in activities such as hobbies or physical exercise. This also involves the capacity to regulate any emotional outbursts that may occur while doing the task at hand. If you have the ability to self-regulate, you can maintain your composure in stressful situations rather than allowing your urges to control you.

You have been able to discover the most productive methods to connect to other people thanks to your high level of emotional intelligence. When it comes to communication, having empathy for the other person and understanding of their perspective go a long way. You will stand out as a wonderful person and an amazing leader if you show compassion for the people around you. You will be able to manage your interactions with people in a professional situation by using the abilities that you have acquired. When you are doing performance reviews of your employees, you will be able to offer them their grades while maintaining a respectful attitude. They won't feel self-conscious talking about their work with you at all.

Your confidence will serve you well in your endeavor. You will have the ability to decide things with full self-assurance. The other members of your crew have faith in your abilities to steer the ship in the right direction. They have no problem receiving instruction from you, and they are able to comprehend what you are trying to do.

Inappropriate Behavior In The World Of Business

When I was in the seventh standard, my English teacher took all of the males outside of the classroom to question them after smelling what she believed to be cigarette smoke in the classroom. The males were seen to be "criminal offenders," while the girls were regarded as "innocent beings." She just peered into our faces and judged (taking into consideration the marks that were granted to the students in the English subject, during the examinations that were conducted), and then she got back all of the lads into the class, leaving only five of us outside! English was not my strong suit; nonetheless, I excelled in mathematics and science. In spite of the fact that the other four were renowned, it was not possible to establish beyond a reasonable doubt that someone from our group had smoked. However, as a kind of punishment, the instructor had us stand outside of the classroom as though we were abandoned. By the way, while on general patrol, our school's principal saw us and took note of what we were doing. He communicated with us. He was aware of the situation and inquired with the instructor about our admission. The decision made by the instructor was incorrect. She made the mistake of relating her academic success to her own characteristic characteristics, and as a result, she came to the incorrect conclusion. The principal of the school was absolutely correct. He made his choice, which was not influenced by bias, and went with social analytics. Irrational human beings often have limited worldviews, which leads to a biased and affected mental process. As a result, their perceptions get skewed, and they make poor choices. If this kind of decision making were to become widespread inside the company, it would put the expansion of the business in jeopardy.

From a psychological point of view, a biased mental state may be attributed to a person's personal history, cultural history, belief system, experience obtained during life, professional conception, and other factors. In addition, having a biased mindset leads to making prejudiced decisions, which are almost always incorrect. The process of making decisions need to be open to public scrutiny and ought to provide convincing justifications. When making decisions in the business environment, protocol calculus should be applied.

LEARNING FOR THE COMPANY Do not attempt to match an employee's personal characteristics with their professional profile. Take an objective rather than a subjective stance! The employee facilitation process should not rely on deceptive maneuvers but rather on a straightforward professional examination.

The Dictation, The Tempo, The Pitch, The Tone, And The Volume

What we say is responsible for the transmission of a significant portion of the data that we share. Do not, however, fall into the trap of believing that the information that our message transmits is sent by the words that we select to use. The manner in which we convey information to our audiences is much more important than the actual words that we employ. Our dictation, in addition to our speed, divulges a great deal of personally identifiable information. The tonality, tone, and loudness of our voices convey a tremendous lot of information about how we now feel about whatever topic is being addressed. The capacity to "read" other people's speech by analyzing their tempo, pitch, and volume is innate in all of us; nevertheless, learning to dictate requires additional practice and instruction.

Dictation, together with accurate pronounciation and proper enunciation, will make things lot simpler for your audience, enabling them to concentrate on what you have to say. If you want to be understood by as many people as possible, practice making your statements more straightforward by cutting out words that aren't essential.

Put some effort into properly stressing the phrases you choose; this helps to portray emotion and truly drives home the point you're trying to make.

Words per minute are the standard unit of measurement for pace or speaking rate; however, syllables per minute may also be used in some circumstances. This is something that naturally changes from language to language, but for the sake of this discussion, we will focus on English and an average word count per minute. According to research done on the speech patterns of experienced public presenters, the optimal number of words per minute ranges between 150 and 180, depending on the circumstances. Changing the pace at which you talk during a discussion, presentation, or pitch can assist to attract and keep audience attention, and as a result, will contribute to the overall impression that people have of your charisma. When you're working toward mastering your speaking pace, it's important to pay attention to the level of difficulty of the information you're conveying as well as the clarity of your vision and language.

Pitch is something that we usually have a fair deal of control over; nonetheless, in order to achieve a complete sound from your vocal chords, it is essential that they retain as much moisture as possible. In addition to drinking plenty of water before a public speech (or even just every morning before you leave the home!), try humming for a few minutes while altering the pitch and tone of your voice. When you speak in front of an audience, your vocal range will expand thanks to the voice warming effects of this exercise.

A pleasant tone of voice is comforting because it lets you know that the person you are speaking to can be trusted and that you can rely on them. In order to cultivate a friendly tone, you must first identify the sorts of tones that sound pleasant to you, and then you must start to reflect the types of tones that are compatible with your tone and accent. Eliminating the regional slang from your vocabulary is one way to become more comprehensible if you have a heavy accent.

When speaking from the heart, it is important to slow down and use a tone that is somewhat deeper than normal. This will help others understand the significance of what you have to say.

When you talk, you should ideally want to be heard by the people around you. Do not yell at the top of your lungs if you need to boost the volume of your voice; this will just strain your vocal chords, making your voice sound hoarse. If you need more volume, talk firmly from your diaphragm by tightening the muscles in your stomach and lower back. Doing so will provide more depth to your voice, allowing it to travel farther without compromising the quality of your tone of voice or the content of your message.

Turn your back on the crowd.

Some individuals get into the habit of not looking directly at their audience while they are speaking in front of them;

instead, they can stare at the ground, a light, or an empty seat. However, this behavior in and of itself displays a lack of self-assurance and a lesser value. Those who select this way run the risk of missing out on one of the natural applications of their voices; yet, not looking directly at the audience may assist with confidence concerns. while we stare at another individual, our voices instinctively change pitch so that they are better able to hear us while we are speaking. This allows the other person to better understand what we are saying. Take use of this innate ability that you possess.

A buzzing sound

Every morning and before making any kind of public presentation, the voice need to be warmed up so that it is ready for action. Warming up your voice is not only for singers. Beginning with a low, deep pitch while paying attention to the sensations occurring inside your chest is a good place to start. After humming at a low volume for a few seconds, gradually increase the pitch by one or two steps and continue doing so every five seconds.

Gymnastics for the Tongue

Not only are tongue twisters an excellent method to hone our elocution abilities, but they also help us improve our memory and boost our self-assurance.

What to eat and drink

It goes without saying that we need to consume a lot of water in order to keep our bodies from being dehydrated. In addition to drinking water, you may try soothing your voice chords by mixing in some lemon and honey, and drinking herbal tea is also quite effective.

Steer clear of anything that might irritate your throat, such as carbonated beverages, alcohol, energy drinks, fruit juices, and anything else that contains caffeine. Because they cause an increase in phlegm production, dairy products also have a negative impact on the quality of our voices.

Spicy meals are very effective in breaking up the phlegm that naturally accumulates in our throats, which may sometimes make a person's voice sound hoarse or as if it is being pushed.

Although it should go without saying, it is important to point out that smoking causes substantial harm to our throats and vocal chords, and quitting smoking is something that should be given serious consideration. A logical person will not make smoking a habit in their life.

Strategies For Efficient Leadership Of Groups And Teams

One of those tasks that, on the surface, seems to be straightforward is leading a group of people. In actual use, it may turn out to be a very challenging job. In order to become an effective leader of a group, what specific strategies should you implement?

Create a Persuasive Argument Vision that is both imaginative and prescient

To be a successful leader, you need followers. If you want other people to follow you, you need to be able to create a clear picture of what the future will probably be like and why they need to be a part of building this wonderful future. If you don't do this, your hearts and ideas will never engage with one another.

Accept Yourself as You Are

Because you are a human, you will have some powers at your disposal. These may take the form of skill, experience, or insight; they might also take the form of particular attributes. Concurrently, it's possible that you have other places that aren't as powerful. If you have these insights, you will not only have a better grasp of the situation, but you will also be able to better direct where you focus your time and effort and figure out the composition of your own team as a result.

Learn more about the members of your team.

I'm usually shocked by how much work we make into finding out about the shortcomings and strengths of new recruits, such as the fact that we only spend a fraction of that time studying our current personnel. I'm always startled by how much attention we put into finding out about the weaknesses and strengths of new hires. Having a good understanding of your team allows for more accurate job and responsibility assignment. It is also likely that this may aid with motivation, since it will make it easier to assign tasks that excites them.

Set Aside Specific Objectives

Goals that are too vague will lead to outcomes that are sub-optimal at best, and non-existent at worst. To achieve your objectives, you should be as detailed as you possibly can. Focus on guiding them to action-oriented and hang time restrictions as your primary objective. You may, if you like, separate them into more manageable milestones along the way.

Put your focus on establishing trust.

If a team does not have adequate faith in its ability, it might end up failing. There are instances when it is simple do things that increases trust, such as living up to one's promises or treating everyone the same.

Keep people accountable at all times.

The fact that the leader continually lets individuals off the hook is perhaps the part about the team that is the most discouraging. Obviously, there will be times when there are legitimate primary reasons why someone cannot achieve what they promised. Concurrently, there may be those who consistently under-deliver on what they promise, just due to the fact that they are aware that there would be no follow-through.

Employ Your Mouth and Ears in the Appropriate Ratio in Order to Succeed

To put it another way, you and the other members of your team need to work on improving your ability to pay attention to one another. My impression is that individuals struggle the most when it comes to the skill of listening. Bear in mind that you only have one mouth while having two ears.

The conclusion is that achieving success as a leader is not guaranteed; nonetheless, there are a few basic elements that may have a significant impact on your level of success as a leader of a group.

Giving Your Team More Agency

You, as the leader, are aware that your team functions very efficiently, much like a well-oiled machine. You want them to have the highest possible rate of productivity so that they can be of assistance to you in achieving your goals for your company. One of the most important factors in making this a reality is giving people agency.

If you read this chapter carefully and use the advice that is provided below, you will learn how to do just that. This may also make it possible for you to identify who among the members of your team is one of the shining lights. You could even choose out a potential future leader.

Let's have a look at the following recommendations for enhancing the level of empowerment enjoyed by team members, all of which should be implemented immediately.

Encourage the sharing of thoughts and perspectives with one another.

One of the finest things you can do is make it possible for the people of your team to talk to you about their thoughts, ideas, and observations. Because of this, you will have the ability to consider all of your choices and make an informed decision. If this turns out to be a solid concept for the firm, how will it help the company?

Inspire the people of your team to investigate more and articulate the idea's potential benefits. Which result do you foresee taking place? Foster open communication and debate, and remember to always pay attention when it's required.

Offer constructive criticism.

It is gratifying to get favorable comments for a work that has been successfully completed. As the leader of the team, it is your duty to see to it that the members of your team are appropriately rewarded for their contributions. Nothing makes individual members of a team happier than being acknowledged for their contributions and successes.

As a direct consequence of this, individuals will see an increase in both their level of confidence and their output. Because they are confident in their ability to succeed at what they do.

Serve as an example for them to follow.

You have the chance to serve as a mentor to individuals of your team who are committed to being with the organization for the foreseeable future. It's possible that others are gaining experience in their field by working for you. You may be of service to someone who has approached you for aid or direction by supplying them with the right resources and tools when they make such a request.

They will look to you as the one to whom they should turn to solve any difficulties when it is time for them to move on. Especially when they have established themselves as independent leaders.

Develop future leaders.

You have the ability to help someone who you believe has the potential to someday take on a leadership role in the organization. One strategy is to find someone who is more qualified than you are to handle the tasks and projects that have been assigned to them.

Give them responsibility for the many tasks that you wish to see through to completion. That individual will have the perception of being a valued contributor to the team. Make sure that they are already doing a good job in the role that they already hold.

There will be less work for you to do. On the other hand, it will provide that great player the chance to demonstrate their worth in a capacity that is different from the one they now play.

Maintain an open-door policy at all times.

Any good leader knows how important it is to keep the lines of communication open at all times. In the event that any of the members of your team have inquiries, remarks, or concerns, here is the place to voice them. This might contain things like ideas, the goals of a firm, different initiatives, and so forth.

Give individuals the opportunity to voice their opinions towards business in general. If things don't seem to be going well for them, you may also provide them an ear to vent their frustrations to. At the same time, lead them to the tools or resources that they need in the appropriate location.

For instance, if someone is experiencing burnout or mental health concerns, you may assist them in taking time off to relax, recoup, and reestablish the mental state that is necessary for them to resume being productive.

Have trust in the members of your team. If you have faith in the ability of your team to do the task at hand, they will undoubtedly feel the same way about you. Your other players will be looking to you to establish goals, make plans for the future, and guide the road forward. They have faith in your capabilities as a leader, and as a consequence, they place their confidence in you.

You provide that trust in return, and the members of your team will advocate on your behalf one hundred percent of the time. They could have the idea in their heads that they would give their lives for the cause that you are heading, if that makes any sense.

The people in your immediate environment will reap significant rewards if you empower your team. They will experience joy, a greater sense of appreciation, and an increased willingness to carry out the task if you ask them to.

It is also quite important that you take part in the decision-making process and that you communicate this information to them. Especially in situations when significant choices about the organization need to be taken. Nobody likes it when things are altered without their being informed beforehand.

One thing that no leader should ever forget about is their team, and that includes themselves. Without them, it would be very difficult, if not impossible, for them to accomplish their goals.

The Driven And Enthusiastic Leader

Imagine being part of a team where the person in charge isn't really enthusiastic about the job that they perform. Because it is possible that all of the other members will also be unmotivated in this case, a great leader should be enthusiastic about the objective as well as the process of getting there in order to inspire their followers.

When a person believes in something with every fiber of their being, they will experience the powerful feeling known as passion. A person's passion is what propels them to keep moving ahead and committing themselves fully to their trade. If the leader of a team who is enthusiastic about what they do shows that passion, the rest of the team will be driven to feel the same way and will perform at a better level.

It is indisputable that passion is something that can never be coaxed out of a person; hence, each person need to constantly have vision and purpose statements that are articulated in a manner that is both clear and compelling. These will assist rekindle the fire of enthusiasm that served as the impetus for beginning the project in the first place. Someone who is devoted to these statements, who lets this dedication reflect on performance, and who inspires the rest of the group to do the same thing is an example of someone who might be considered a passionate leader.

The Process of Becoming One:

Those that have the deepest degree of dedication to the accomplishment of the team's objective are the most effective leaders. Use these techniques to reawaken the desire that lies dormant inside you:

Achieve success by your own internal drive. Motivation may be either internal or extrinsic, depending on what drives an individual. Someone who is studying to become a doctor because of the prestige that comes with the profession is an example of someone whose drive to achieve anything is extrinsic. Extrinsic motivation is when you are inspired to do something due of external factors. On the other side, intrinsic motivation is when you want to become a doctor because you are compelled by a strong desire to serve the needs of other people. Spend some time thinking about why you want to pursue something, and if you find that you are solely driven by things outside of yourself, make an effort to change your motivation so that it comes from inside.

Maintain an open mind and heart for candid conversations. Allowing everyone in a team to talk about how they feel about a particular project is the most effective method to get everyone excited about working on that project. Before beginning the conversation, establish some clear ground rules, such as waiting for one person to complete speaking before turning the floor over to the other. The person who is now holding the talking stick should not be stopped while they are in the middle of expressing themselves, but they are required to hand it over to another member of the group once a certain amount of time has elapsed. Certain group leaders have a talking stick that is passed around the group.

Make your commitment public and clear. Your commitment will be etched in stone once you let everyone know that you are on board with the initiative one hundred percent, and it will motivate others to participate one hundred percent as well. People tend to become more dedicated and impassioned once they are aware that all eyes are on them, therefore there is also a significant difference between fulfilling a commitment to yourself and informing the world about it.

Because their work is something they actually care about, leaders who are driven by passion take complete delight in their work. Put yourself in a position to inspire others and bring about significant change by surrounding yourself with a group of people who share your level of enthusiasm and commitment.

You Really Need To Have Passion.

First and first, you have to be passionate about what it is that you are doing or what it is that you are attempting to achieve. A significant number of leaders lack enthusiasm. They are just thinking on the benefits, such as money or privileges, that may come from having the job. They are woefully ignorant of how vital it is to invest their hearts and minds in their job and communicate that enthusiasm to the members of their team.

Think at it this way: if you do not feel enthusiastic about what you are doing, what is the point of continuing to do it? And how could you possibly expect other people to be interested if they realize that you are not enthusiastic about the subject matter yourself?

If it isn't already clear, one of the keys to success is to follow your interests. If you are just starting out in the business sector, for example, you should search for a profession that will not only allow you to maintain your current standard of living but will also encourage your mental and spiritual development. If you like what you're doing, it won't seem like work even when things become challenging. Love what you do. It will be much simpler for you to get to the position of outstanding leader from here on out.

With a fervent...

You will assist other people in understanding that it is OK to pursue what it is in life that they want. Some individuals are of the opinion that they should forget about what it is that they really want and instead make do with what is now accessible. That is not correct. It is necessary for you, as a great leader, to let other people understand that it is OK for them to pursue their aspirations. A great leader is someone who motivates people to be true to who they are in spite of the challenges they face. If someone is honest with themselves, they will have more chances to improve themselves, and as a result, they will be able to motivate and encourage others around them.

You won't have the feeling that you're "working," but you'll still perform to the best of your ability no matter what you're doing. When you are engaged in an activity that you are enthusiastic about, it seldom seems like labor. It's a lot of fun to try your 'best shot' at anything. Pressure is transformed into excitement, expectations into objectives, and accomplishment into a sense of accomplishment and satisfaction.

You will have a sense of satisfaction and joy. Imagine that you have a passion for cooking and decide to build a restaurant of your own, or at the very least, begin working right away toward launching a restaurant someday. You won't consider this endeavor to be work at all since you have such a passion for the kitchen and because you are always seeking for new methods to improve your culinary techniques or come up with delicious new dishes. In this manner, not only do you get to work with what you love, but you also have the opportunity to share your abilities with the world, which will ultimately lead to a sense of accomplishment and satisfaction on your part.

You will become an expert in the activity that you are engaged in. Naturally, if you like what you are doing, it will be much simpler for you to perform to the best of your abilities. You start to wonder about it. Your expertise and knowledge base will grow, which, in turn, will fuel your excitement and motivation.

Great outcomes open doors to previously unimaginable possibilities. Your outcomes will mirror the level of enthusiasm you put into whatever it is that you are working on while such feelings are present. Never settling for less than their best, great leaders always start with excitement and passion for the work they are doing. They provide the greatest outcomes as opposed to results that are simply "okay"; if you are able to accomplish this consistently, more people will respect and appreciate you, and more people will be eager to follow you as a consequence.

Keep in mind that it is really crucial to be enthusiastic about the job that you do, not just in this day and age but particularly in this day and age.

Remember it, and you won't veer from the path that leads to success!

Next, it is time to discover how you may communicate to your subordinates in the appropriate manner, which will allow you to have the most productive conversation possible; additional information about this will be provided in the next chapter.

Social Skills

Being a competent manager, managing the office, and the management abilities that this activity demands are not the only aspects of leadership that are important. It is essential for a leader to have strong social skills in addition to strong managerial abilities. This is due to the fact that the leader is a social person who spends a significant amount of time engaging in conversation with people from all walks of life in the community. As a manager, he is seen on the shop floor interacting with the machinists. As the chair of the company, she is seen in the boardroom with senior management personnel. As a social activist, she is seen in public spaces advocating for a social cause. As a politician, he is seen in meetings with other political leaders forging a bill. As a magistrate, she is seen in the courtroom pronouncing judgments that have profound effects on the lives of litigants.

At each and every one of these events, the leader is obligated to exhibit his social abilities, which are also often referred to as social graces. A person's social skills may be described as the art of successfully navigating themselves within social groupings. A person's style of speaking, eating, gesturing, clothing themselves, and walking are just a few examples of the kinds of talents that fall under this category.

The setting of the social event, the goal of the event, and the individuals that make up the social group all have an impact on a person's level of social competence. Therefore, the social skills needed for a get-together with friends will be different from those needed for a party hosted by the workplace.

Followers' social behavior is often determined by how their leader behaves in society; in the majority of circumstances, the leader serves as the role model for society. People in the field of fashion and movies are the ones that set the trend with their costumes, and the designs of these outfits are then made accessible in shops for the followers to buy. This is why fashion magazines and movie magazines have such a large fan following. Mahatma Gandhi is an additional illustration of the role of the leader in forming the preferences and feelings of the people in a society. Gandhi's demonstration of the art of non-violence as a method for resolving conflicts was adopted by Martin Luther King Jr. during the civil rights movement in the United States, and then again by Nelson Mandela during the process of bringing an end to apartheid in South Africa.

Therefore, in this part of the discussion, we will have a look at a few of the social abilities that characterize the personality of a leader and position him or her at the forefront of a social grouping.

Personal Representation

People follow leaders because they have a unique trait that's referred to as "force of personality." Due to the fact that this is an abstract characteristic, it is famously difficult to describe. However, it is possible to explain it. Let's give that strategy a go in this particular segment.

Magnetic personality.

A leader exudes a distinct presence that captivates the interest of those around her. "Charisma" is one term that may be used to describe this inner aspect of mystique. It is the act of a person projecting an undefined and abstract characteristic in such a way that others are drawn to that person as a consequence of that projection. A person's charisma may be attributed to a number of different factors. The individual could have specific characteristics that distinguish him apart from other individuals, such as complete honesty, for example. There are numerous situations in which we are either partly honest or completely dishonest, despite the fact that the majority of us are honest in general. Nevertheless, the secret to certain leaders' appeal is their unwavering commitment to being completely truthful. One such individual was the Prophet Mohammed, who was renowned for his unwavering integrity. As a result of this reputation, people felt comfortable entrusting him with their belongings when they went away on long-term business ventures, knowing that their valuables would be returned to them in pristine condition when they returned from their journeys. The total commitment that some political leaders have to the betterment of society is the source of their charm.

Hygiene of the individual.

When it comes to conveying the persona of a leader, personal cleanliness is a crucial factor. A leader is expected to have a tidy appearance. Take note that those who hold positions of spiritual authority and who are able to command large followings usually present in a tidy and clean manner. Even if they wear a beard, it is never wild or unkempt but is instead maintained in perfect control at all times. The ancient adage that

"Cleanliness is next to Godliness" has undeniably some truth to it.

The elimination of body odor is the next most important component of good personal hygiene, after cleanliness. A natural byproduct of certain people's skin, body odor may be caused by a broad variety of factors, including poor hygiene and eating patterns, as well as conditions that affect the skin. Others give off body odor as a result of the perspiration that their bodies produce; in especially in tropical climates, sweat is a substantial emanation from the skin as a result of the heat and humidity that exists in such regions. The production of sweat may also be attributed to the effects of effort. Because so many individuals don't properly care for themselves, their bodies give out unpleasant odors. No matter what the reason may be, the effect of having a strong body odor is that it has a tendency to make other people avoid you.

Therefore, maintaining a high level of personal cleanliness is an essential part of developing the social skills necessary to become a leader. Showering once each day is recommended for maintaining personal cleanliness. After a shower, the mind will feel more refreshed because the water from the shower washes away the dirt and filth that have settled on the body, opens the pores of the skin so that more oxygen can penetrate it, and cleans the body of the dust and grime that have settled on it. It is important to wash one's hair on a regular basis in order to maintain it clean and free of dirt and filth; this is especially important for aspiring female leaders with long hair who choose to leave their hair in its natural state. The facial hair of male leaders who choose to retain beards should be washed frequently and, if they are not self-conscious about doing so, trimmed so that they provide a tidy appearance. It is strongly recommended that a deodorant be worn, regardless of the environment, since the clean aroma of a deodorant is pleasant and welcoming to both the wearer and others around them.

Getting ready.

Shakespeare once remarked, "The apparel oft proclaims the man," which means that others make assumptions about us based on the clothing that we choose to wear. As a result, a leader need to absolutely create a fashion statement with his or her choice of attire.

Take heed that we are use the term "style" in this context, and not the term "fashion." The term "fashion" refers to the most recent trend, and trends change constantly. Some styles do last for a considerable amount of time, however the vast majority of trends only last for a short while. On the other hand, style is the individual's own clothing statement; it only identifies the individual's individuality. You could take one or two aspects of a fashion trend and incorporate them into your own unique style, but ultimately, you should create something that people will appreciate and want to emulate.

Shakespeare had a lot of insightful things to say about life in general, and one of those things was what a person ought to dress. Polonius advises his son Laertes in Shakespeare's play Hamlet, as Laertes is getting ready to leave for France to further his education, "Costly thy habit as thy purse can buy, But not expressed in fancy; rich, not gaudy; For the apparel oft proclaims the man...."

If you want to make a fashion statement, following Shakespeare's suggestion, you do not need to dress in costly garments; instead, select clothes that are within your price range. Your clothing should have an opulent appearance without being over the top. You have a colorful style, yet it's not garish at all.

How you dress should be determined by the environment in which you will be wearing it. Dressing for the workplace is one category, dressing for a get-together with friends is another, and dressing for a trip with coworkers is still another.

We would like to provide you with a slogan for your fashion sense, and that mantra is "Elegance."

Theories Regarding The Continuum

The universalist theories fail to take into account the intricacies of leadership behaviors, whereas the contingency theories do. For instance, they presume that theories of leadership need to take into account the elements of both the environment and person variations. In addition, they stress the importance of the fact that a leader's capacity to lead or influence his subordinates at work is contingent on his ability to adjust his leadership styles to a variety of scenarios.

a) The idea of leadership based on situational analysis

Two distinct patterns of behavior are distinguished by the framework that Hersey and Blanchard created. They are referred to as "relationship behavior" and "task behavior," respectively.

The level to which a leader participates in two-way communication with their subordinates is what is meant by the term "relationship behavior." It involves the degree to which subordinates are supplied with emotional supports and encouraged, as well as other behaviors that facilitate their work.

The term "task behavior" refers to the degree to which superiors provide subordinates with direction and advice, including telling them what to do, how to do it, and when to do it.

Both of these behaviors may be found, although to varying degrees. As an example, the manager may demonstrate more task-oriented behavior than relationship-oriented behavior, or vice versa.

Henry and Blanchard, on the other hand, came up with four fundamental leadership styles by combining the behaviors associated with tasks and relationships. They are the

High workload and little interpersonal connections = telling style

High levels of both activity and connection equals the selling approach.

Participating style is characterized by a low level of task and a high level of connection.

Large amounts of work with little interpersonal connections = delegation style.

According to them, the four styles are only useful in certain contexts, and the degree of maturity of the individuals who report to them determines how successful they are. Maturity level refers to an individual's capacity and desire to accept responsibility for his or her own actions in this context. A subordinate may do well on a particular job, and as a result, need less supervision in that area; yet, his performance may be bad in another area, and as a result, he will require supervision in that area until he develops.

b) The Leadership Contingency Model [The Leadership Contingency Model]

Fred Fiedler's (1976) contingency theory is widely regarded as one of the most compelling explanations for the world we live in today. According to what it states, the efficiency of a group's performance is a product of the interplay between the leadership style of the individual in charge and the favorable circumstances (also known as the environment). The following are the three environmental factors that he considers as interacting with different leadership styles in order to determine how successful leadership is:

a) boss-member relations — This refers to the degree to which subordinates have faith in and respect for their boss. It is possible to determine whether or not the leader is accepted by their subordinates and whether or not they get along well with them. Editors and other managers in media organizations that have positive relationships with the employees under their supervision find it simple to influence those employees, and those employees have a high esteem for the managers.

b) Task structure - this relates to the degree to which the task objectives and responsibilities assignment are described in a clear and concise manner. The manager should inquire as to whether or not every subordinate is aware of what has to be done by asking the pertinent inquiry. Is there room for interpretation in their line of work? Which objectives are there to be accomplished? How exactly can one get them?

c) Position power is a kind of power that relates to the official authority that a leader has. The ability of leaders to employ both incentives and punishments effectively will directly correlate to the amount of influence they have. The managing director of an organization has more discretion over who receives incentives and who gets disciplined than his subordinates do. On the other hand, the manager's authority to recruit and dismiss employees as the head of the department is far stronger than that of his subordinate.

(c) The Model of the Path and the Goal

This concept, which was developed by Robert House, operates under the presumption that the actions of leaders may have an effect on the performance of subordinates on the job by demonstrating to them how their actions might contribute to the accomplishment of collective objectives. The expectation theory of motivation is used as a foundation for this approach. For instance, it emphasizes the idea that effective leadership behavior leads to increased goal achievement by subordinates and even clarifies the pathways that lead to those objectives (i.e. expectation).

If employees think that they are capable of performing the assignment using their own initiatives, a leader may refrain from engaging in directive behavior or providing direction in order to encourage the pleasure of subordinates in the job achievement. Their level of pleasure will increase as a result of this behavior, in contrast to the level of discontent that would be caused by directives behavior, which is needless.

Clarification of the qualities of the job as well as the expectations associated with it is still another component of the model's purpose, which is to decrease ambiguity. When work tasks are clearly defined, there is less room for doubt about whether or not a goal will be accomplished; this makes it easier to visualize achieving the objective. In addition, when normal occupations are given a dose of diversity in the form of new tasks to do, working becomes more fulfilling and reduces irritation.

Take Advantage of Their Predilection for Computers and Socializing With Others

You have to go on to the next part of the process after you have successfully built a strong connection with your Millennial employees, provided them with opportunities for advancement, and begun to leverage their talents. The next step is to capitalize on their amazing affinity for modern technology and networking.

This is the procedure that should be followed to complete this phase.

Include the Technology that they are using in their Workplace in yours.

Organize a meeting with your millennial workers and ask them about the many technical devices, software, apps, and developments they use in their personal or professional lives. Additionally, ask them how you can incorporate these technologies into the working environment. This conference is going to be pretty significant for your professional life, and it is going to assist you in bringing about a revolution at your organization.

For example, if you have no experience with Pinterest or any of the other social media forums that may assist you in advertising and promoting your company, you can consult with Millennials about how to boost marketing strategies by making the most of these platforms. You will be able to make use of their enthusiasm for technology in this way, which will give them the impression that they play a significant part in the operation of the business and encourage them to put in even more effort.

Leverage their enthusiasm for making connections.

Engage in conversation with the millennials who work for you and bring them along to a variety of social and professional activities. Because of this action, you will enhance your reputation as a leader and forge a closer connection with the millennials who make up your workforce, both of which will be to the great advantage of your organization.

People Are The Most Important Aspect Of Leadership

Everyone is affected by this, unless your business is entirely automated and only deals with other automated businesses. People are the most crucial aspect of your business model, regardless of whether your firm is governed by people or whether it sells to people. This is true regardless of whether scenario applies to your organization. Therefore, they are entitled to be shown the highest possible regard.

If your workers believe that they are respected and appreciated, they will put in 10 times the effort that they would put in if they believed that they were devalued and utilized. "People Quit Bad Bosses, Not Bad Jobs" is the subtitle of this book, and it couldn't be more accurate.

In my experience in the military, I saw a number of instances in which decent soldiers deserted their posts because of abusive superiors. This has a domino effect and will snowball. individuals will leave an organization because of a poor manager, and the more individuals that leave, the more work the remaining workers will have to do; as a result of the increased workload, some of these workers will decide to leave the company as well. When this happens, the corporation is forced to pay out of its own funds to educate more employees. Avoid having this occur in your firm by demonstrating gratitude to those who have helped you.

Action: Have someone schedule a day for the team to connect, such as a trip out to go racing or paintballing, and then follow it up with a supper together afterward. If you wish to, you may take care of the organization yourself.

If you can find someone to organize everything for you, that person may include it in their annual report to demonstrate that they are capable of getting things done.

The eighth lesson is that it is okay to acknowledge when you've made a mistake.

Everyone has a fallible human nature, and it is only normal for people to sometimes make errors. One of the most important qualities of a successful leader is the capacity to admit when they are wrong and accept responsibility for their actions. Don't point the finger at anybody else or make an effort to cover it up. People have tried to cover up their blunders in front of me before, but it always ends up being a larger issue. To put one's hands on one's head and admit, "I was wrong," needs a person of considerable stature and a great deal of guts; to do so in front of one's whole workforce requires an even greater person.

If you demonstrate by raising your own hands, it will be much simpler for your colleagues to follow suit. It is far simpler to correct an error when it is caught early on, before it has had the chance to snowball into a much more serious issue. It is simpler to cope with these kind of circumstances if you just come out and say what you need to say rather than sitting down for a significant amount of time. Therefore, you should simply walk out in front of all of your workers and lift your hands up by doing this. Keep in mind that you are leading by example and bringing some of the other principles of strong leadership skills into action by doing this.

Take Action: There is not a whole lot more to say about this other than the fact that you should accept your faults sooner rather than later.

The ninth lesson is that together we are strong.

The power of 10 minds is greater than the power of one mind. Employees have provided some of the most innovative ideas for some of the largest firms in the world, and it helps businesses function more effectively when their staff is cohesive.

I have noted in the past how our manager took the time to sit down with all of us and address both the positive and negative aspects of working there. This is a principle that should be followed by all businesses, regardless of their size. It is your responsibility as a leader to bring the members of the workforce together.

Take action: Make it a goal to have at least one meeting a week or once a month just for the purpose of having staff members communicate their thoughts and concerns. If you accomplish this, you will strengthen the cohesiveness of the staff, leave employees with the impression that they are cherished and appreciated, and make improvements to your business.

To me, this is such a no-brainer that the only possible outcomes of these meetings are positive ones; thus, you should go into work tomorrow and schedule the first meeting of the staff.

The outing for team building may also be an effective technique to bring the workers closer together.

The tenth and last point is that there is always space for improvement.

The expansion of both the company's operations and its revenue should be the primary focus of every business, regardless of its current size. There is no such thing as a flawless firm, and there never will be; regardless of how large your operation is, there is always opportunity for development. Employees are also included in this category of people.

Training and mentoring your staff will be beneficial to the organization, so be sure to provide them with these opportunities. All of these things—keeping employees in the firm, being an effective leader, showing your employees that you support, respect, and value them, and making them feel valued—contribute to a robust corporate culture.

This also refers to 'yourself.' A wise guy once advised that you should invest at least 10 percent of your annual salary in your education.

Keep in mind that a leader is someone who helps workers get better and encourages them.

Implementing a training program for your employees may help enhance the quality of their job as well as provide them with a general education.

Make arrangements to attend a class so that you may improve your own education.

Increase the amount of time you spend reading, particularly non-fiction.

Educate Yourself On The Traditions Of The Working Environment

Another thing that a great leader should bear in mind is how essential it is to have a deep comprehension of the culture that their organization has. You need to have an understanding of the kinds of things that the people around you desire, as well as the reasons why a certain product or service succeeds in a particular culture but fails to succeed in others.

People's means of making decisions, the way they talk and interact with one another, the tales they tell their children and grandchildren, the myths and legends that are passed down, and the methods of doing labor are all fundamental components of culture. It is also about the customs and traditions of a certain location or nation; but, in this case, we are speaking about the culture of your place of employment.

It is also believed that culture is something that can be learnt and that it reveals a great deal about the behaviors of the people who live in a certain location. The thing that really counts is that you have to grasp the culture of a certain location in order to know what you might provide to the people there and to know more about the people who are already around you.

This chapter will teach you everything about how to understand your culture and create the greatest sort of goods and services for your people. There are specific methods in which you could understand your culture, and you'll discover all about those ways.

Taking a Look At

The first thing you need to do, just like everything else in life, is to observe your culture since doing so will allow you to embrace and comprehend it. This is just like everything else in life. To do this, you need to:

Take a look at the activities going on in the area around you. Check out what others have displayed on their workstations or walls, observe what they are wearing, and make an effort to learn what it is that they enjoy to listen to or watch in their spare time. In this manner, it will be simple for you to comprehend what has a possibility of working and what does not, and it will be simple for you to devise goods and services that will be beneficial to the individuals concerned.

Observe the behavior of your followers in their interactions with one another. You will have an understanding of what drives them or what causes them to become agitated in this manner. As you can see, the people around you are pretty much a representation of the individuals you would want to follow you or purchase your goods, and as a result, it is very crucial that you know what they want and what they do not want.

Look for hints that aren't being spoken. You read in a previous chapter about the significance of non-verbal communication; you should focus on improving this skill. You should educate yourself not only in the art of nonverbal communication for yourself, but also in the art of interpreting the nonverbal communication of others who are in your immediate environment.

Taking Stock

The next thing you need to do is take inventory of the area around you. You are able to do this by asking certain sorts of questions, such as those that will help you better understand things and will be able to guide you toward making a decision about what it is that you could do. The following are some examples of possible questions:

Where exactly are all of the many departments that make up your office located?

What kinds of things do individuals keep on their workstations?

What are some common topics of conversation during breaks?

What do individuals talk about in their e-mails and letters to one another?

How often do individuals use their phones, other electronic devices, and computers?

How would you characterize the tenor of your messages? How do you communicate with other people? Do you present a welcoming demeanor or do you intimidate them?

What kinds of movies and television programs do they like watching? Which songs are now enjoying a lot of success?

What kind of garments do they put on their bodies?

What can you notice hanging on the walls or posted on the bulletin boards?

What kinds of foods do individuals like eating?

What kinds of things do individuals do in the various regions of your office?

What kind of reactions do people have toward you and toward one another?

What exactly are the contents of your memos?

Discussions Through Interviews

You are aware of how crucial it is to conduct interviews with potential employees before employing them and incorporating them into your business, right? Well, interviews are also crucial if various individuals are already working in your firm, so that you would know how people are getting along with each other or if there is anything that needs to be changed. This would allow you to know how people are getting along with each other and whether or not something needs to be changed. inquiries like as, "Who do people consider to be a "hero" or someone worth emulating around the office?" are examples of sample inquiries.

If there was one item in the workplace that needed to be altered, what would it be and why would it need to be changed?

Which values do you feel are most essential for your employees to uphold? How would they want to see these values reflected in the work that they perform and how would they like to see it done?

Do they believe that these ideals still have significance in today's world?

What do you think is the most impressive aspect of the organization?

What do you think is the most impressive quality that the employees possess?

Why do certain errors occur, and how can we stop them from happening in the future?

What is the single most telling sign that the business won't succeed?

Re-organization of Cultural Practices

You'll be able to determine whether or not any kind of change is required after carrying out interviews and doing an analysis of the current state of affairs. Reorganization of cultures is possible via the following means:

Having an understanding of the culture that you presently have and basing your future endeavors on what you have picked up from the people in your immediate environment are two important steps. As this is a significant choice, you should keep in mind that you should not decide on your own and instead solicit the feedback of those who report to you.

Make a decision on the direction you want to take your firm, as well as the qualities or services you would like it to represent. Consider the ways in which this new vision might benefit the firm as well as the ways in which it can be compatible with the culture that you are now a part of. Testing your ideas in the market is very necessary in order to determine whether or not they have a chance of being successful in the long run.

Ask yourself what you may be able to do with this new vision, and then inquire of the people who follow you about their reactions to it. If none of you have any reservations about it, then you should go with the mission; but, if you get the impression that the majority of your followers are uneasy about it, then you should call off the expedition since it is unlikely to be successful.

And make the necessary adjustments to your conduct so that others will be inspired to do the same. You, as a leader, should be the one to initiate the change. You should have faith that this shift will result in positive outcomes and that it is feasible for you to achieve your goals if you all put in the necessary effort.

Observe, evaluate, and conduct interviews before attempting to reorganize your culture. This will ensure that you get the most accurate picture possible. Don't be in a hurry to make a choice.

www.ingramcontent.com/pod-product-compliance
Lightning Source LLC
Chambersburg PA
CBHW050420120526
44590CB00015B/2039